THE
CONTEMPORARY
READER

VOLUME 1, NUMBER 5

CB
CONTEMPORARY
BOOKS
CHICAGO

Contents

If you had lived in the 1860s,
do you think you would have wanted
to ride for the Pony Express?

THE 2,000-MILE RIDE

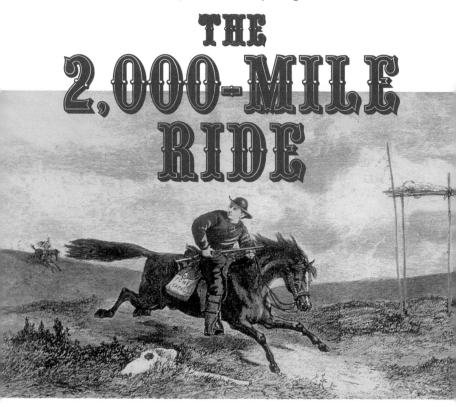

HELP WANTED

1   **Young men without families. Hard work. Long hours, night and day. Dangerous. Lonely. Must not be afraid of snow, floods, or wild animals. No drinking or swearing. Pay: $100 a month.**

2   Would you apply for a job like this? More than 200 young men and boys did. They rode for the Pony Express.

THE WILD WEST

3   In 1860, the eastern part of the United States was home to many people. From the Atlantic Ocean to the Mississippi River, there were many cities and towns. Two thousand miles to the west was California, where many other people had settled. But between the Mississippi River and California were 2,000 miles of emptiness.

4   The Wild West was still wild. It stretched over mile after mile of wide grassy plains. There was dry, dusty desert, and after that, high mountains.

5   It took months to get from the East to California. Some people traveled by horse and wagon along rough trails. Others took stagecoaches, which bumped along all day and night. The track was so rough that stagecoaches could cover only 100 miles in 24 hours.

6   The trip was always dangerous. Many people died of sickness or lack of water. Others were killed by American Indians who were fighting to keep their land. At best, people were

freezing cold in the winter and covered with dust in the summer. The West was a hard place in which to live.

7   Like everything else, the mail was slow. By stagecoach, it could take two months for a letter to reach California from the East. Even the most important news had to wait. The stories in California's newspapers were always at least a month old.

FAST HORSES

8   Then some businessmen had a great idea. They would send the mail across the West on fast horses. They thought people would pay well to get letters through quickly.

9   The businessmen spent $500,000 to set up the Pony Express. They built 190 stations, 10 to 15 miles apart, all the way from St. Joseph, Missouri, to Sacramento, California. They bought 500 of the best horses. Then they hired 80 riders. The riders were young—many of them only boys. But the smaller the better! The average age of the riders was just 18.

10   Each rider was given a Bible. The riders were not allowed to drink or swear. They carried the mail in waterproof bags on their saddles.

A Pony Express rider dashes off on a fresh horse for his 75-mile trek westward.

11   The first rider would start from St. Joseph and ride as fast as he could to the first station. The keeper at the station had a fresh horse all ready for him. The rider would jump off his horse, grab the mailbags, and jump on the new horse. He was gone again in less than two minutes.

12   A rider was to cover 75 miles and then pass the mail to the next rider. But if the next rider couldn't take over, the first rider had to push on.

SPEEDY SERVICE

13 The riders carried the mail 250 miles in a day—much faster than the stagecoach could. They also took a shortcut. They used the same track as the stagecoach as far as Salt Lake City, Utah. But then they went due west, through the desert and over the mountains. This route saved them 100 miles, but it was more dangerous.

Folk hero "Buffalo Bill" Cody rode for the Pony Express when he was only 14 years old.

14 The Pony Express could get the mail from St. Joseph to Sacramento in only eight or nine days. The fastest trip was in November 1860, when the Pony Express carried the news that Abraham Lincoln had been elected president. But the Pony Express was no bargain. It cost $5 to deliver a half-ounce letter. This was at a time when the best-paid riders were making $3 a day.

RAIN, SHINE—AND DANGER

15 The riders braved every kind of weather. Each one carried two guns and a knife to protect himself from wolves, panthers, and other attackers. Each rider was all alone, on his own, as he dashed along the track to the next station.

16 Even with all the dangers, the riders almost always got through. In all, they rode 650,000 miles, and the mail was lost only once!

17 More than 200 riders worked for the Pony Express. Some famous men in history, such as "Buffalo Bill" Cody and "Wild Bill" Hickok, got their start riding this route. A Pony Express rider had to be fast and had to know the West well. Above all, he had to be fearless.

DOOMED DELIVERY

18   The Pony Express seemed like an exciting way of life. But it was gone almost as soon as it had started. Something new quickly took its place. It was a yet faster way to get the news across the country. This invention was the telegraph.

19   During the 1850s, telegraph lines were being strung all over the East. In 1856, many telegraph companies came together to form the Western Union Company. They soon began putting up lines in the West.

By 1861, the telegraph could wire news across the country in an instant.

20   One crew started at the Mississippi River and worked west. They put up poles, strung wire, and built telegraph stations. Another crew started in California and worked eastward. Between them, the Pony Express route became shorter and shorter.

21   The two telegraph crews met at Salt Lake City on October 24, 1861. The telegraph wire stretched from coast to coast. News could travel across the country in an instant. It meant the end of the Pony Express.

22   The businessmen who started the Pony Express lost all their money. Although this service lasted only 18 months, the Pony Express stands out among the daring achievements in our history. And we remember the brave, lonely riders of the Wild West to this day. ♦

QUESTIONS

1. What were some of the dangers a Pony Express rider faced?

2. By stagecoach, how long did it take a letter to reach California from the East?

3. What was the fastest trip the Pony Express made? Where did the trip begin and end?

4. What put the Pony Express out of business?

5. For how long did the Pony Express run?

Does classic art mix with rock 'n' roll? How does a famous architect bring them together?

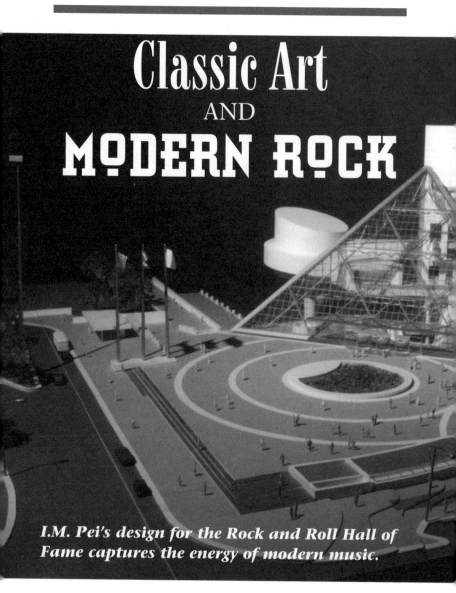

Classic Art
AND
MODERN ROCK

I.M. Pei's design for the Rock and Roll Hall of Fame captures the energy of modern music.

1   The Rock and Roll Hall of Fame in Cleveland, Ohio, is made of simple shapes. Start with a pyramid, a cylinder,[1] and blocks within the structure. Then add large amounts of glass. Now you can understand the style of I. M. Pei [Pay].

2   Pei is a famous architect[2] [ar'•kih•tekt]. Why he first came to the United States and how he developed his style make an interesting story.

HIS CHILDHOOD

3   Ieoh [Ee•ay'•oh] Ming Pei was born in 1917 in the city of Canton, now called Guangzhou [Gwang•jow'], China. His father was a bank manager who was sent to open a new branch in Canton. But the fierce fighting among the local

---

[1] cylinder: a round figure with two flat ends

[2] architect: one who designs buildings and gives advice on their construction

I. M. Pei poses in front of the Louvre, for which he would later design a new entrance.

warlords[3] made life dangerous. So the bank sent the Pei family to Hong Kong and later to Shanghai [Shang•high'], China.

4   As young Pei grew up, buildings held great interest for him. He studied the old-style buildings of China's countryside. He studied the first skyscraper built in Shanghai. Early in his teens, he knew he wanted to design buildings.

COMING TO THE UNITED STATES

5 In 1935, Pei came to the United States to study architecture. His fellow students couldn't pronounce his name. So they called him "I.M."

---

[3] warlords: forceful military leaders

Now almost everybody uses that nickname. He received a degree in architecture from the Massachusetts Institute of Technology in 1940.

6   Pei had planned to return to China then. But World War II had begun, so he stayed in America. In 1942, he married Eileen Loo. She was also Chinese-born and an architecture student. She went on to study landscape architecture at Harvard. Pei began graduate work there also.

7   In 1943, Pei left school to join the war effort. He worked for the National Defense Research Committee. His job was to find ways to *destroy* buildings! The following year, he returned to Harvard.

PEI'S TEACHERS

8   At Harvard's Graduate School of Design, Pei had two famous teachers. Walter Gropius [Grow'•pee•uhs] had led a school of design in Germany before the war. He stressed simple shapes. Marcel Breuer [Mar•sell' Broy'•er] had a strong interest in light and shadow. Both Gropius and Breuer taught that "form follows function." That is, the form of a building should depend

on its use. Pei's work still shows the effect of these two great architects.

9   Pei completed his master's degree in 1946. But China was still unsafe, so he stayed in the United States. He taught at Harvard for two years. Then he worked for a New York real estate developer. Pei designed housing projects and office buildings around the country. He made each building fit with the buildings around it. This work gave him valuable experience.

HIS OWN BUSINESS

10 In 1955, Pei became a U.S. citizen and started his own design firm. The range of his projects grew. They included a chapel and a government center. He designed university buildings and an airline terminal. People began to notice Pei's special style. He received awards for several of his buildings.

11   In 1964, Pei was asked to design the John Fitzgerald Kennedy Library in Boston. The space was small, but the building had to look big. As Pei said, "It represents the importance of the presidency." His design joins a cube, a cylinder, and a triangle. The building is mostly concrete

Pei gave the John Fitzgerald Kennedy Library in Boston a stately look within a small space.

and glass. This project brought Pei attention from all around the country.

MORE PROJECTS

12 Pei and his partners became busier than ever. They designed libraries and museums, hotels, a hospital, concert halls, and banks. These projects took Pei's firm all over the world.

13 Two of Pei's favorite projects brought him back to his homeland. One was the Fragrant

Above: The Louvre Museum of Art in Paris, France, challenged Pei with its classic look.
Right: Pei's award-winning pyramid design for the Louvre entrance shocked everyone.

Hill Hotel near Beijing (formerly Peking). The hotel combines traditional Chinese styles and materials with modern ones. The other project was the Bank of China skyscraper in Hong Kong. This is the bank for which Pei's father had worked.

14   In the United States, Pei's most famous project is in the nation's capital. It is the east

wing of the National Gallery of Art. The new building's design had to fit in with the old museum. Pei designed two triangle-shaped buildings. He blended the different styles, sizes, and materials of the three buildings into an exciting whole.

15   Another design for a museum won him worldwide fame. Pei created a new entrance for

the Louvre [Loov] in Paris, France. He wanted the design to be modern, yet have a classic look. Pei chose a pyramid of steel and glass. At first it shocked many people. Then they decided that the pyramid was perfect.

AWARDS

16 I. M. Pei can be proud of the many awards he has won. In 1986 he received the U.S. Medal of Liberty. This goes to foreign-born citizens who have contributed to American life. In 1989 he won the Praemium Imperiale [Pray'•mee•oom Eem•pair•ee•ahl'•ay]. This is a new award from the Japanese Art Association. It honors lifetime achievement in the arts. Worth $100,000, this prize is as highly regarded as the Nobel Prize.

ROCK 'N' ROLL

17 Since 1989, Pei has chosen to work on smaller projects. The buildings may be small, but they are just as exciting as his larger works. An example is the Rock and Roll Hall of Fame in Cleveland, Ohio. It is located at North Coast Harbor on Lake Erie.

18   A 165-foot tower rises from the water. At one side, a slant-roofed block juts out 60 feet over the water. At the opposite side is a cylinder.

It appears to be balanced on the other end of a seesaw. A seven-story tent of glass slants away from the tower onto the land. Pei meant the design "to echo the energy of rock 'n' roll."

19   At first, it seems an odd couple—rock 'n' roll and a man born in imperial[4] China. But I. M. Pei has never been bound by the past. Nearing the age of 80, Pei keeps his work bold and surprising. ♦

Questions

1. Who is I. M. Pei, and where was he born?

2. What is special about Pei's designs?

3. Which of Pei's buildings was the first to bring him national attention?

4. Where is the Rock and Roll Hall of Fame?

---

[4] imperial: relating to an empire or emperor

What is inside a volcano? Is there a way to warn people about volcanoes' danger?

WHEN THE EARTH ERUPTS

1   In the year A.D. 79, a volcano blew up in Italy. It destroyed the city of Pompeii. The entire city was buried under 15 to 25 feet of ash.

2   Now the city of Pompeii has been dug up. You can visit it and see the people lying the

A 1902 eruption in Martinique wiped out a city of 30,000 people, leaving only two survivors.

same way they fell. As they ran from the volcano, the ash covered them. It made casts of their bodies. The casts make it seem as if that awful moment from 2,000 years ago had happened only yesterday.

MELTED ROCK

3   Much of Earth was formed by volcanoes. Below its surface, Earth is hot enough to melt rock. The melted rock is always moving. It has cracked the earth's surface into about 20 large pieces called *plates*.

4   In some places, the plates are being pushed together. One plate gets pushed below another and begins to melt. As the rock melts, it creates hot gas. Pressure [presh'•er] builds up under the surface. The melted rock begins to push up through a crack in the earth's surface. This movement is an eruption.[1]

5   Sometimes the melted rock, called lava [lah'•vah], flows out. Lava is red-hot. Its temperature is above 2,000 degrees. It can flow down a mountain at 60 miles an hour!

HOT GASES

6   At other times, the gases build up under the earth until they cause an explosion. Ash and rocks burst into the air. The top of a whole mountain can blow off in a few seconds.

7   The blast can release hot gases that quickly flow down the mountain. The gases are so hot that they burn everything in their way. When Mount Saint Helens in Washington state blew up in 1980, the blast destroyed trees as far as 17 miles away!

---

[1] eruption: a bursting forth or breaking through a surface

Red hot lava from an eruption burns up a house. Melted rock can move up to 60 miles an hour.

UNDER THE OCEAN

8 Volcanoes are always changing the shape of the earth. Most of the time, we don't see the changes because they are hidden deep under the world's oceans. Underwater volcanoes send melted rock flowing out onto the ocean floor. The rock cools and hardens, forming new mountain ranges under the water.

9   Sometimes, though, we see a sudden change in the shape of the earth. The Mount Saint

Helens eruption blew off the top of the mountain, leaving a huge crater.[2] The mountain is much shorter now.

10   But 10 years earlier, on the other side of the world, something different happened. Off the coast of Iceland, a volcano built up a new mountain in the middle of the ocean. The mountain became so tall that it stuck out of the water and formed a new island.

Some Good

11 Surprising as it may sound, volcanoes do some good. The ash blown out of the volcano falls to the ground and covers many miles. This ash contains everything that plants need for growth. On the island of Java [Jah'•vah], for example, there are many volcanoes. People there are able to grow three crops every year.

The Dangers

12 But volcanoes can be deadly. In 1985, in Colombia, 23,000 people were killed by a wave of mud from a volcano.

13   In 1902, a volcano in Martinique [Mar•tin• eek'] sent hot gases into a city, killing 30,000

---

[2] crater: a bowl-shaped hole around the opening of a volcano

people. Only two people in the whole city survived. One of them was lucky enough to have been in a room with very thick walls—it was a jail cell.

14   In 1815, in Indonesia [In•doh•nee'•zha], a volcano blew up and killed 12,000 people. It destroyed so much of the land that 80,000 more people died of hunger. Ash blew 17 miles into the air. Because of it, a cloud covered the whole Earth and kept out the sun, lowering the Earth's temperature. People in the United States called the following year the "year without a summer" because snow fell during June, July, and August.

In October 1983, Hawaii's Kilauea [Kee•lah•oo•ay'•ah] volcano roared into action.

This Colombian volcano's blast killed 23,000 people only a week before this picture was taken.

ACTIVE VOLCANOES

15 There are 550 active volcanoes on Earth today. At least a dozen of them are erupting right now. And 500 million people live close enough to volcanoes to be in danger. Further, those that haven't erupted for hundreds of years could suddenly reawaken.

16 We cannot stop a volcano. But we're learning how to know *when* to get out of a volcano's way. Keeping an eye on volcanoes around the world is a risky job. A number of scientists who monitor[3] volcanoes have been killed by blasts of hot gas or even by eruptions.

---

[3] monitor: watch or check for a special purpose

17   Their work has been useful, though. In 1991, a volcano erupted in the Philippines. It killed 900 people and destroyed 42,000 homes. But there could have been much more damage. People in the area were warned before the volcano erupted. Because of the warning, 200,000 people were moved away from danger.

18   Scientists still don't know exactly when a certain volcano will erupt. It could be days or months or hundreds of years from now. In the meantime, people who live nearby go on with their lives. How do they do it? Maybe they simply try not to think about it and hope for the best. ♦

QUESTIONS

1. What can visitors see in the city of Pompeii?

2. What is lava?

3. How do mountain ranges form underwater?

4. What can be good about volcanic ash?

5. How many active volcanoes are there?

6. Why is it important for scientists to keep track of volcanoes?

What deep anger causes a man to take another's life? What four U.S. presidents were the victims of such anger?

SOMEONE SHOT THE PRESIDENT!

1   Abraham Lincoln was the 16th president of the United States. He was the first to be assassinated.[1] But he was not to be the last.

APRIL 14, 1865

2   The Civil War had been over only days. President Abraham Lincoln was ready to enjoy a night out. He and his wife arrived at Ford's

---

[1] assassinated: murdered by surprise or secret attack

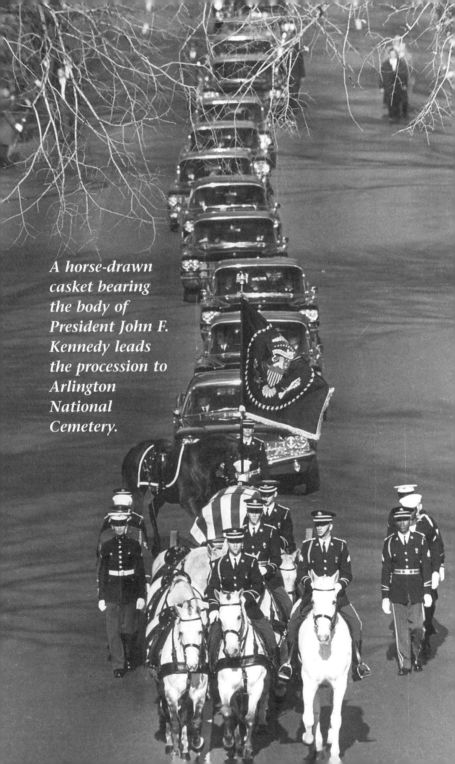

A horse-drawn casket bearing the body of President John F. Kennedy leads the procession to Arlington National Cemetery.

Theatre in Washington, D.C., to see the play *Our American Cousin*. Joining the Lincolns were Major Henry R. Rathbone and his guest. All four were led to their seats in a special box 12 feet above the stage. A bodyguard stood at the door of the box.

3   The president seemed to enjoy the play. During the third act, the bodyguard left his post. Just as Mary Todd Lincoln took her husband's hand, a man entered the box. He had a gun in one hand and a knife in the other. Aiming carefully, he shot the president in the head. Lincoln fell forward. Mrs. Lincoln screamed as she caught her husband.

THE STRANGER ESCAPES

4   Rathbone reached out to help. But the stranger used his knife to slash the major's arm. The attacker then leaped toward

Above: John Wilkes Booth shoots President Lincoln as he attends a play at the Ford Theater.
Left: Booth then leaps from the box to escape.

the stage. His boot spur caught on the flag that hung across the box. As he fell, he broke a leg.

5   The audience watched it all in horror. The attacker wasn't a stranger. He was someone they

had seen on that very stage—an actor named John Wilkes Booth. Even with a broken leg, Booth ran out of the theater before anyone could catch him. Outside, a horse was waiting. Booth hopped on and got away.

No Hope

6 Lincoln lost consciousness [kahn'•chus•ness]. Six soldiers carried him to a house across the street. Five doctors worked all night trying to save him, but it was hopeless. A bullet had entered his head, behind the right eye. Early the next morning, Lincoln was dead.

7 The funeral was held in the White House four days later. On April 21, a train set out for Springfield, Illinois, to take the dead president home. John Wilkes Booth was tracked down. He had escaped to Virginia and was hiding in a barn. Booth was shot and killed on the spot. What was his motive?[2] Some believed he was unhappy that the South had lost the Civil War. Others said it was a plot, and that other leaders were to be killed as well. The full story about Lincoln's death may never be known.

---

[2] motive: something that leads a person to commit an act

Before the final try, Charles J. Guiteau had planned several earlier attempts on President Garfield's life.

JULY 2, 1881

8 President James A. Garfield was on his way to attend his 25th class reunion at Williams College in Massachusetts. He also planned to enroll his two sons as students there.

AN ANGRY PERSON

9 Garfield had been in office for less than four months. He had been naming people to serve in high offices. A battle raged over who these officials should be. A man named Charles J. Guiteau [Ghi•toe'] was sure that he had the

skills needed for one of the jobs. Guiteau was often seen at the White House waiting to talk to Garfield. But the president refused to see him.

10   Guiteau was very angry—angry enough to kill. He had almost succeeded in killing Garfield before. One time Guiteau tried to shoot Garfield in a church. He tried another time while the president rode in a carriage. In a third instance, Guiteau waited for Garfield in an alley near the White House, but still he did not follow through.

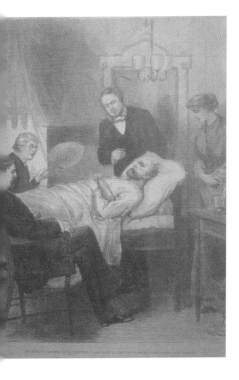

Far left: Seized just after shooting President Garfield in the back, Guiteau was hanged a year later. Left: The gravely wounded president lies in his room at the White House.

THE FINAL TRY

11 Guiteau learned of the train trip that the president and James G. Blaine, the Secretary of State, would take to Williams College. Guiteau followed the two men to the Pennsylvania Railroad Station in Washington, D.C. When Garfield and Blaine walked by, Guiteau quickly came up from behind. His first shot hit Garfield's arm; his second struck Garfield in the back. The president was still alive but gravely wounded. He hung on for months and later that summer left the White House for his home in New Jersey. He died there on September 19, 1881.

12 Guiteau was hanged on June 30, 1882.

Above: Leon Czolgosz shoots President McKinley at close range inside the Temple of Music.
Right: Czolgosz hated government and was angry enough to kill.

SEPTEMBER 6, 1901

13 William McKinley, the 25th president, was not far into his second term. He appeared to be a strong leader with high hopes for making the United States a world power.

A WELL-LIKED PRESIDENT

14 The American people were fond of McKinley. Although his wife was ill, he was a kind and happy man. He had many friends, but he also had a serious enemy. Leon Czolgosz [Chohl'• ghosh] hated government and, most of all, hated the president. In Buffalo, New York, McKinley was visiting the Pan-American Exposition.[3] Czolgosz was there as well.

15 The day before, during a speech, the president had spoken about trade among Pan-American countries. He talked of building the Panama Canal. At the Temple of Music, hundreds of people waited to shake his hand.

A TRAGIC SCENE

16 Leon Czolgosz waited in the crowd, a gun in his right hand. A bandage covered it from view. As soon as he came close to McKinley, he pulled the trigger. Once again, the president didn't die at the scene. He was taken to the home of the person in charge of the exposition. Eight days later, on September 14, President William McKinley was dead. Czolgosz was executed on October 29, 1901, at Auburn, New York.

---

[3] Pan-American Exposition: a 1901 event designed to highlight a century of progress in the New World

President John F. Kennedy, Jacqueline Kennedy, and Governor John B. Connally ride through Dallas moments before the assassination.

NOVEMBER 22, 1963

17 The 35th president, John F. Kennedy, was in Dallas, Texas. He had come to take part in some speeches to win the confidence of the people. Kennedy and his wife, Jacqueline, were in the backseat of an open automobile. Governor John B. Connally and his wife sat in front with the driver. Large crowds along the streets waved and cheered as the auto passed by. The people seemed happy to honor their president.

Heavy snow and freezing temperatures can last as long as eight months.

place because there isn't much wind in Willow. That's a help in winter as well as in summer. There is no strong wind to knock over or break any of the tall flowers.

12   The climate is almost arctic[3]—it stays cold and dark for many months. A year ago, the average temperature from the middle of October through December was 0 degrees. Once the snow fell in October, the ground was covered with snow until May. Winter is so long and forceful here that some describe summer as "the beautiful lie." The ground is very cold. Sometimes, it doesn't warm up until the middle of June. Last year Brake had ice in his flower bed until June 8.

---

[3] arctic: relating to the north pole or the region around it

Alaskan white nights give an unusual, ghostly glow to garden flowers and plants.

NATURAL BEAUTY

13 As Les Brake says, the best reason for gardening is the natural beauty of Alaska. One friend can see glaciers[4] [glay'•shurz] from his garden. Another has Mount McKinley for a background in her garden. Somebody else he knows gardens by a lake that reflects the nearby mountains.

---

[4] glaciers: large, slow-moving bodies of ice in a valley or on a land surface

And Brake himself gardens in the foothills of mountains. There's a spruce forest around his house, and to the side of it, a pond.

LONG WINTERS

14 Brake's greatest challenge as a gardener is getting through the long winters. He reads gardening books and magazines. He meets friends at the local garden club. He also enjoys growing bulbs in pots indoors. That way, he can also have flowers in the winter.

15 In April, the Great Land starts to wake up from the long winter. As this happens, Brake is more excited with each passing day. Here, in America's last frontier, Les Brake feels that he's helping to create a special kind of garden. ♦

QUESTIONS

1. Why did Les Brake move to Alaska?

2. How long does the summer sun last?

3. What helps to keep moose away in the summer?

4. How many inches of snow fell in the last two winters?

Camels can go for days
without water.
How can they do it?
And what is really inside
those humps?

MADE FOR THE DESERT

1   For thousands of years, people in desert countries have used camels. Camels can carry heavy loads and pull plows. Camels provide clothing, shelter, food, and milk. To sum it up, camels are perfect for desert life.

Strong Legs and Feet

2 Camels are built for the desert. Their long, strong legs move easily over the uneven ground. They move slowly, only 3 miles an hour, but keep going on and on. A camel can

travel about 25 miles a day and carry up to 1,000 pounds.

3   Camels are sometimes called "ships of the desert." You might not want to ride on a camel, though. As they walk, the legs on each side move together, making the camel rock from side to side. The swaying movement could make a rider seasick!

4   A camel's feet hold up well, even in soft sand. Instead of having hooves like a horse, a camel has two toes on each foot. Each toe is protected by a toenail, and between the toes is a large pad. As the camel steps down, the pad spreads out. The pad keeps the camel from sinking in the sand, just

Their strong legs and feet make camels the ideal beasts of burden.

A camel grazes on a light lunch of dried leaves and twigs.

the way snowshoes keep a person from sinking into deep snow.

Special Eyes

5   The desert can be a dusty place, but dust is no problem for a camel. Its eyes have three eyelids. The outer two eyelids work like ours, having curly eyelashes to keep out the sand. An extra

thin eyelid on the inside can close to wash dust off the camel's eye. Its big eyebrows stick out from its head and shade the sun.

6   A camel's ears are small and set close to the head. Hair on the inside as well as the outside of the ears keeps out the sand. The camel can keep sand out of its nose, too. Its nostrils are just slits. In a sandstorm, special muscles close the nostrils tightly.

THE CAMEL'S HUMP

7 In the desert, food and water can be hard to find, but camels do just fine. They can go for days without drinking water, and even longer without food.

8   How does a camel do it? Many people think a camel's hump is full of water, but a camel's hump is really a big lump of fat—80 pounds of it. The fat stores energy for the camel to use when there's no food. This means a camel can go for days or even weeks with no food at all. If the camel doesn't eat, the hump begins to shrink. It might even flop over and hang down on one side. As soon as the camel eats, the hump again begins to fatten up.

A Good Appetite

9   Luckily, camels are not picky eaters. They eat just about anything, including dry leaves and seeds. Camels even eat cactus without getting hurt. The inside of a camel's mouth is so tough that the cactus thorns don't bother it. If there are no plants around, camels can eat meat, fish, or even bones. Like cows and sheep, camels chew their cud.[1] This gives them time enough to grind down what they eat before their bodies digest it. But camels' owners have to be careful. A hungry camel might chew on its bridle or even its owner's clothes!

---

[1] cud: food brought back up into the mouth by some animals to be chewed again

Above: A festively clothed camel lays down its burden for the day.
Left: Camels will eat a cactus—thorns and all.

No Sweat

10 So how does the camel go without water? A camel gets much of the water it needs from its food. In the winter, when the weather is cool, the plants the camel eats contain plenty of moisture. So it may not drink any water at all.

Camel rides by the sea are a tourist attraction.

11   In summer, a camel needs about five gallons of water a day. But a camel can manage without water for several days. How? They do it by not sweating. Unlike camels, people have to keep their body temperature even. If a person's temperature goes up just two or three degrees, it's a sign of illness. On a hot day, sweating helps to keep body temperature steady. But it doesn't bother a camel if its temperature goes up, even as much as 11 degrees. Because a camel doesn't sweat, it doesn't lose water.

GOOD AND BAD

12 Camels are truly useful animals. They're strong enough to carry heavy loads over rough ground.

Their hair is thick and sturdy, and when it falls off in the spring, it can be woven into blankets and tents. Camel meat tastes something like veal. And camel milk is so rich that if you put it in your coffee, it becomes lumpy.

13 The only problem is that camels can be very bad-tempered. They groan and complain when they stand up under a heavy load. They sometimes spit at their owners or kick them suddenly. They're useful and perfect for the desert. So what if they sometimes show their bad temper. You would, too, if you had to carry the burdens that they do! ♦

QUESTIONS

1. How many miles can a camel travel in one day?

2. What is stored inside a camel's hump?

3. Why can a camel go for so many days without water?

4. How many eyelids does a camel have?

5. What do camels do that might anger their owners?

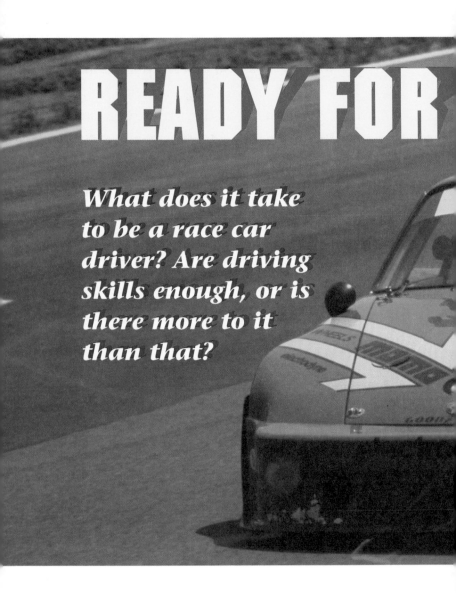

READY FOR

What does it take to be a race car driver? Are driving skills enough, or is there more to it than that?

1 The track at the Indianapolis 500 Speedway is 2¹/2 miles long. At speeds of about 250 miles per hour, you can whip around the track in about

HIGH SPEEDS

38 seconds. You make a left turn, then drive a short straight stretch. After another left turn, there's another straight run, then you must turn

left again. The track is packed with other cars. At any moment, a car could cut in front of you and crash into the wall. Or you could crash. You make another left turn, and go into the straight!

2   Then you do it all again—199 more times—as fast as you can push your car.

STAYING CALM

3 What kind of a person do you have to be to drive a race car? One thing you need is nerve—and plenty of it. At 250 miles per hour, a crash is never more than a split second away. You're driving a car that's being pushed to the limit. The engine is turning 10,000 times per minute, hour after hour. Most cars used for street driving would blow up if pushed past 7,000 turns per minute. The wheels, the clutch, or any part of the car could let go at any moment. But you stay calm and dive into the next turn.

4   The human heart beats about 75 times per minute. During a race, a driver's heartbeat jumps up to 160, even 180! At the Indianapolis 500, a driver gets a bit of a break during a yellow flag. That's when the track is cleared after a crash. But in races like the Grand Prix [Pree], a

Drivers need a cool head and keen wits when racing at top speed.

driver's heart hammers at 180 beats per minute nonstop for two hours!

No Rest

5   Most people would feel completely exhausted. But you can't rest during a race. Race car drivers have to train their bodies. Formula 1[1] drivers' average heart rate while resting is down around 63 beats per minute. Their bodies also make better use of the oxygen they breathe. This means that even at their high heart rate during

---

[1] Formula 1: a racing car of a certain size, weight, and engine power having a long, narrow body; open wheels; a single-seat open cockpit; and a rear engine

a race, drivers still have energy left at the end of races. And they may need it if their cars' steering starts to wear out.

GOOD SHAPE

6   Drivers also have to be in good shape. Body fat takes blood away from the brain and muscles. It also keeps the body warm. In a hot race car, an

overweight person would feel too warm. Drivers also need to be able to bend their bodies easily. They will less likely be hurt in a crash if their bodies can bend.

7   Good eyes are another "must." Drivers have to see things that are far away and be able to quickly judge how far away they are. They also

have to see close-up things, like the oil gauge [gayj]. Drivers also must be able to see things clearly out of the corners of their eyes. Drivers need this kind of vision to see, for example, a wheel come off the car to the right.

REACTION TIME

8   Seeing objects ahead of time isn't enough. A driver has to decide what to do about what he or she sees—and do it—in an instant. How fast a person can act is called *reaction time*. Anyone who drives a car needs good reaction time, but in a race, a driver has

A sleek Formula 1 race car is perfectly crafted to handle high speeds.

Drivers take time before a race to get their cars and their minds ready to win.

to think much faster. Even one-hundredth of a second can make a huge difference. At 200 miles per hour, that split second equals a whole car length!

9   A driver can test his or her reaction time on a machine. On the machine, eight buttons are set into a desktop shaped in a half circle. The driver has to hit the buttons that light up, one after the other. The buttons are wired to a computer, which counts the driver's reaction time. Indianapolis 500 drivers are very quick. Formula 1 drivers, who must race on turning, twisting roads, are even quicker.

MARIO ANDRETTI

10 Drivers have to be able to concentrate on the race—and keep on concentrating. They can never let up. Mario Andretti [An•dre'•tee] wrote about the first time he won the Indianapolis 500, in 1969. By the 110th lap, he was a whole lap ahead of all the other cars on the track. All he had to do was keep his car on the track for 90 more laps, and he would win. But twice he almost lost it. First, on the 150th lap, he was thinking about everything except what he was doing. He got too close behind another car. Caught in its draft, he flipped sideways and found himself headed straight for the wall.

11 The second time, toward the end of the race, Andretti forgot for a moment what he was doing.

Veteran race car driver Mario Andretti waves to his fans.

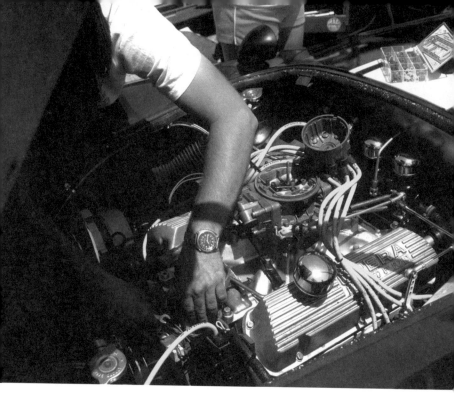

Drivers must keep their cars, bodies, and minds in top shape to win.

At 200 miles per hour, a moment is a long time! Again he almost drove into the wall. After that, he said, he kept his head—and won the race.

A GOOD ATTITUDE

12 One more thing race car drivers need is a good attitude. They have to go into races with the idea that they're going to win. Some drivers do this by thinking back to times they have felt the best, the most ready, and the most confident.

They set their minds to feel the same way again. They take time before a race to get their minds ready for racing.

13   When you think about it, these sound like good tips for succeeding at just about anything. Stay calm. Concentrate. Think fast. Keep an eye on everything that's happening around you. Keep your body in good shape. And whatever you do, keep a good attitude. With all this going for you, how could you lose?

14   One more thought comes from Grand Prix winner Jacky Ickx. He says that his greatest races were not always the races he won. They were ones in which he felt a personal triumph [try'•umf]. The real winning is inside yourself. ♦

QUESTIONS

1. How long is the track at the Indianapolis Speedway?

2. Why is reaction time important in race car driving?

3. What happened to Mario Andretti when he didn't keep his mind on driving?

THE TRADE-OFF

Gangs and guns were a way of life at San Francisco's Geneva Towers.

How did tenants of a San Francisco apartment building help turn a dangerous place to live into a safe one?

1 Geneva Towers was the most dangerous housing project in San Francisco. Gangs shot at one another. When the police came, the gangs threw garbage at them. The police were pinned down by sniper fire.

2 Not anymore. Geneva Towers is clean of drug traffic, gangs, crime, and even graffiti[1] [gruh•fee'•tee]. The story of how this happened shows us some things.

3 First, a dangerous housing project *can* be made safe. But it takes a lot of force. Second, the price is high in two ways. It costs a lot of money. And people must sacrifice[2] some freedom to be rid of fear.

TAKING OVER

4 The story began on June 6, 1991. That day, a federal government agency took over Geneva Towers. The agency was the Department of

---

[1] graffiti: messages or drawings written on some public surface

[2] sacrifice: give something up for the sake of something else

Housing and Urban Development (HUD). It had decided that the two buildings were unsafe.

5   HUD hired the John Stewart Company to run the buildings. The John Stewart Company had turned around small housing projects before. But it had never worked in one as big as Geneva Towers. Each of the two buildings has 19 floors. Together there are 576 apartments. Eight hundred people live there.

6   Mari Tustin works for the John Stewart Company. The plan for Geneva Towers was simple. She said, "You secure[3] it, and you clean it up. And you do it instantly."

GARBAGE AND GANGS

7   The cleanup job at Geneva Towers was huge. Heaps of garbage and broken glass filled the lawns. Graffiti covered every wall, and most of the windows were boarded up. The garages were filled with abandoned cars. Gang members hid their guns and drugs in the cars.

8   When workers came to clean up, about 50 residents helped. They took away 90 trash bins of junk. They towed away more than 100 cars. They put in new windows and steamed the

---

[3] secure: to make safe from intruders

graffiti off the walls. But keeping the graffiti off the walls turned into a war. The workers would clean the walls during the day. And at night, the gangs would sneak back again. This went on for months. Finally, the gangs got bored and stopped.

9   Getting rid of the gangs caused another war. The gangs ran every floor in both buildings. They ran the garages, the lobbies, and even the sidewalks. The John Stewart Company hired a private security company. They sent Eli Gray to deal with the gangs. Gray had been a casino bouncer in Las Vegas.

Eli Gray used tough tactics to bring peace and safety to Geneva Towers.

Keeping the graffiti off the walls of Geneva Towers became a war of wills.

THE CRACKDOWN

10 Geneva Towers had 15 guards, who were paid the minimum wage. Only one shift out of three had guns. Gray heard that some guards sold drugs in the building. So he fired most of them. He then hired 60 new guards and paid them more. They all have uniforms. They also have guns, nightsticks, and spray cans of Mace. They wear bulletproof vests.

11   Gray made other changes. All tenants now enter each building through one room. If the guards don't know them, they must identify themselves. All guests must sign in.

Most tenants at Geneva Towers felt it was worth trading some personal freedom for better security.

12   The security company put zoom cameras on the roofs, in the parking lots, and in the halls and lobbies. The cameras send the pictures to a main dispatch room with six viewing screens.

13   A 10-foot fence was built around Geneva Towers. Bright light now floods the halls and outdoors. Buzzers were placed on all the fire exits. If a door opens, it rings in the dispatch room. This tells the guards to watch the screens.

Gang members from 21 cities join hands at a peace conference in Kansas City.

PRIVATE VS PUBLIC

14 Geneva Towers is not a public housing project. It was built by a private company, not the government. This makes a big difference. The guards can do things the law says can't be done in public housing. For example, the guards evicted[4] 70 troublemakers. That would be hard to do in public housing. Also, the guards think of themselves as private citizens. That gives them the right to make citizen's arrests. When they search suspicious[5] [suh•spish'•uhs] visitors and find drugs or guns, they call the police.

---

[4] evicted: forced out a tenant by legal process
[5] suspicious: tending to arouse distrust

15   How far can the guards go? The U.S. Constitution protects people against unlawful search and seizure. Gray says this applies only to search and seizure done by government workers, such as the police. He says it does not apply to search and seizure done by private citizens, like the guards at Geneva Towers.

LEASE CONDITIONS

16 The guards enter apartments if they think there is an emergency. It might be a tip on drug use. It could be a neighbor complaining. Or it could be something suspicious the guards see on the cameras. The police usually can't enter and search a home without a warrant.[6] An exception to this rule is if police are in "hot pursuit" of a suspect. Another is if the police hear the sound of screams or gunfire.

17   Why can the guards enter apartments in an "emergency" without permission? Each tenant's lease is written this way. The lease also says that the landlords can make nonemergency visits, with permission, during reasonable hours. This might be to make repairs inside an apartment.

---

[6] warrant: a legal paper giving an officer the power to carry out the law

The success story of Geneva Towers gives hope to tenants of other crime-ridden housing projects.

18   The law is not clear about how far the guards can go. It does state that citizens may not bother or assault other citizens. This would apply also to the guards. But many other housing projects want to try the plan used at Geneva Towers. And they probably can.

WORTH THE PRICE

19 Dorothy Dean is 70 years old. She has lived in Geneva Towers for 27 years. She says, "It was just like a jungle. The security they got now, I'm so pleased. If they got rid of the security here, I'd be ready to leave." The car of Cornelia Simpo, another resident, was broken into twice.

Now Simpo feels safe. She says the guards "had to rough a few people up, but I don't see any harm in that."

20　　Other residents think the guards go too far at times. They have complained. But Gray says that the guards do what they must to make the project safe. The first year after the guards came, crime dropped. The number of shootings fell from 33 to 7. Violent assaults fell from 66 to 7. In 1993, no major crime was reported in Geneva Towers.

21　　Most of the tenants say they are glad to finally have peace and security. They think it is worth giving up some freedom to be safe. ♦

QUESTIONS

1. Which agency took control of Geneva Towers?

2. Why did Eli Gray fire most of the original guards at Geneva Towers?

3. List two of the changes Eli Gray made to the management of Geneva Towers.

4. Why can the guards enter a tenant's apartment without permission?

Was the Taj Mahal worth the cost and time it took to build?

A Monument Like No Other

1 It rises from the waters of the Yamuna [Yah•moo'•nah] River in India. This grand building is called the Taj Mahal [Tazh Mah•hahl']. It is covered in white marble and set with colorful stone flowers. A pool

A Monument Like No Other 85

reflects the building like a mirror. A large round dome rises into the sky with smaller domes around it. On either side of the main building are two smaller buildings. Both are covered in red sandstone. Each has several domes.

2   This splendid monument can take your breath away. There's the beauty of the whole sight to take in. Then there are millions of fine points to study. Yet, when seeing even pictures of the Taj Mahal you must wonder "Why?"

IN LOVING MEMORY

3   The idea to build the Taj Mahal came in 1631. The emperor of India was Shah Jahan. He was deeply in love with his second wife, Arjumand Banu Begum, who bore him many children. He called her Mumtaz Mahal, which means "crown of the palace." While giving birth to their 14th child, she died. Deeply saddened, the emperor decided to build the finest possible monument to his wife. Mumtaz Mahal's body would rest in a tomb there.

GETTING STARTED

4   The emperor wasted no time getting started. The first step was to find the perfect spot on which to build. He chose the city of Agra, near

Millions of pilgrims honor the Ganges River because their crops depend on its waters.

the Yamuna (or Jumna) River. At that time, visitors entered the country through Agra. The new building would show the world India's best.

5   The next step was to build a grave for Mumtaz Mahal. During the first year, her body was laid to rest in a tomb facing the river. A

dome was quickly built to cover the tomb. Then the rest of the Taj Mahal was built around it.

YEARS OF BUILDING

6   For the next 22 years, Shah Jahan guided the building of the Taj Mahal. He stayed in charge of every step of the work. When finished, the building would be not only the finest in India but also the finest in the religion of Islam.[1] It would give people the feeling of a "heaven on

---

[1] Islam: a religion in which Allah is the only god, Muhammad is his prophet, and the Koran is the holy book

Far left: Visitors first approach the main gate to the Taj Mahal. Left: From inside the main gate, visitors can enjoy a full view of the Taj Mahal itself.

Earth." Beautiful gardens would surround the building. It would be known as one of the seven wonders of the world.

A Closer Look

7   The rounded shapes of the Taj Mahal and its white marble face are what viewers see first. A closer look, both outside and inside, brings the many stone flowers into focus. Made of fine stones of many colors, the flowers look real. Light from the sun bounces off them. They shine in different ways at various times of day.

8   In the Islamic religion, flowers stand for the kingdom of God. Most of the Taj Mahal's stone

flowers are cut flowers, and some are in vases. These stand for the riches of heaven that await those who have faith.

9   A still closer look will show black writing up and down the walls. It is religion as much as it is art. Poems from the Koran, the Islamic holy book, are set for all time into the Taj Mahal.

INSIDE THE ROOMS

10 Islamic holy buildings have eight rooms around one middle area. The main dome of the Taj Mahal has 16 rooms—8 on each of two levels. In the middle area are the tombs of Mumtaz Mahal and Shah Jahan, who died in 1658. The tombs lie side by side, facing east toward the holy Islamic city of Mecca [Mek'•uh].

11   The law of the Islamic religion says there must be a place for prayer near a tomb. So Shah Jahan decided to build a mosque[2] [mosk] beside the new building. The mosque is covered in red sandstone. It has three domes and is smaller than the main building. Once it was built, Shah Jahan decided that the two buildings were not in harmony.[3] So he built a third one on the other side of the main building. He called it

---

[2] mosque: a place of worship in the Islamic religion
[3] harmony: a pleasing or suitable arrangement of parts

Thousands of followers of Muhammad worship here at the largest mosque in India.

Jawab, or the Response, because it looks exactly like the mosque. It is known as the guest house.

ASKING WHY

12 Still, there is the question, "Why?" Did Shah Jahan really build a monument to himself and not his wife? Records show that he was truly saddened by his wife's death. What's more, he placed her tomb in the exact center under the large dome. His tomb, which is off to the side, appears to be a later idea.

A worshipper kneels inside a lavishly decorated mosque. Islam is India's second largest religion.

13   It seems clear, however, that Shah Jahan took his plans far beyond those for an ordinary tomb. He loved buildings. He had built a number of fine ones, including a palace. He used huge amounts of public money to see his dream of the Taj Mahal come to life. He was eager to show it off by placing it for all to see. He even had plans to build a second monument on the other bank of the river. It would be made of black marble. However, it never came to pass because his son put the emperor in prison in his own palace. And that's where he died.

CARELESS UPKEEP

14 The Taj Mahal may never again be as grand as it was while Shah Jahan was alive. Over the years, people stole the silver from the doors. They tore off some of the stonework. And the gardens were left untended. Many people claimed the Taj Mahal was a waste of money.

15 When England ruled India, one English governor wanted to tear down the Taj Mahal. He would rather have sold the materials and kept the money for other uses. In the end, England made repairs to the Taj Mahal. More work has gone into the buildings since India became free from British rule. Still, many say that

Like this Indian man, four-fifths of India's people practice the Hindu religion.

the gardens have never been as fine as when they were first planted.

16   Few parts of the Taj Mahal are actually one-of-a-kind. Nearly all of the domes, the tombs, the carvings, the stonework, and the marble building itself were copied from something else. Yet as a whole, there is nothing in the world like it. The Taj Mahal stands as a monument to Shah Jahan and his wife, to the Islamic religion, and to the thousands of people who worked so hard to build it. ♦

QUESTIONS

1. In what country is the Taj Mahal, and who built it?

2. Why was the Taj Mahal built?

3. Who is buried inside the Taj Mahal?

4. What is the Koran?

5. Why did Shah Jahan build a mosque beside the Taj Mahal's main building?

GLOSSARY

CLASSIC ART AND MODERN ROCK
Pages 12–21
architect: one who designs buildings and gives advice on their construction
cylinder: a round figure with two flat ends
imperial: relating to an empire or emperor
warlords: forceful military leaders

WHEN THE EARTH ERUPTS
Pages 22–29
crater: a bowl-shaped hole around the opening of a volcano
eruption: a bursting forth or breaking through a surface
monitor: watch or check for a special purpose

SOMEONE SHOT THE PRESIDENT!
Pages 30–43
assassinated: murdered by surprise or secret attack
motive: something that leads a person to commit an act
Pan-American Exposition: a 1901 event designed to highlight a century of progress in the New World

GARDENING ON THE EDGE
Pages 44–53
arctic: relating to the north pole or the region around it
frontier: a region that forms the edge of the settled part of a country
glaciers: large, slow-moving bodies of ice in a valley or on a land surface
leaf rollers: insects that make their nests by rolling up plant leaves

MADE FOR THE DESERT
Pages 54–63
cud: food brought back up into the mouth by some animals to be chewed again

READY FOR HIGH SPEEDS
Pages 64–73
Formula 1: a racing car of a certain size, weight, and engine power having a long, narrow body; open wheels; a single-seat open cockpit; and a rear engine

THE TRADE-OFF
Pages 74–83
evicted: forced out a tenant by legal process
graffiti: messages or drawings written on some public surface
sacrifice: give something up for the sake of something else
secure: to make safe from intruders
suspicious: tending to arouse distrust
warrant: a legal paper giving an officer the power to carry out the law

A MONUMENT LIKE NO OTHER
Pages 84–94
Islam: a religion in which Allah is the only god, Muhammad is his prophet, and the Koran is the holy book
harmony: a pleasing or suitable arrangement of parts
mosque: a place of worship in the Islamic religion

THE CONTEMPORARY READER
VOLUME 1, NUMBERS 1-6

The Contemporary Readers offer nonfiction stories—intriguing, inspiring, and thought provoking—that address current adult issues and interests through lively writing and colorful photography.